MY JOURNEY IN GRACE

TYKE CLARK

CITI OF
BOOKS

CITIOFBOOKS, INC.
3736 Eubank NE Suite A1
Albuquerque, NM 87111-3579
www.citiofbooks.com
Hotline: 1 (877) 389-2759
Fax: 1 (505) 930-7244

Ordering Information:
Quantity sales. Special discounts are available on quantity purchases by corporations, associations, and others. For details, contact the publisher at the address above.

Printed in the United States of America.
ISBN-13:   Paperback   979-8-90124-115-8
                eBook   979-8-90124-116-5

Library of Congress Control Number:

Contents

How Far Will I Follow Jesus

"We may have the best intentions to discern God's will, but we should stop putting ourselves through the misery of over-spiritualizing every decision. Our misdirected piety makes following God more mysterious than it was meant to be."
– Kevin DeYoung

1 Peter 2:21 "For to this you have been called, because Christ also suffered for you, leaving you an example, so that you might follow in his steps."

This book is based on the many experiences I have had and the conversations I have had with friends. My wife and I often met with other brothers and sisters on our journey at different locations. When together, we prayed, enjoyed our meal, and had a wonderful time fellowshipping. We discussed many things, shared many testimonies, and discussed our challenges in serving the Lord. This included things that could, sometimes, be a barrier to our commitment to God.

My hope and prayer are that as you read these writings, you will be uplifted as I was inspired as I wrote. I hope they will serve as a beacon of hope as it relates to the many challenges of life that we often face. May you find a new reason for believing again.

When we consider it, Jesus went through a lot for us. Jesus suffered so much on our behalf. Very few of us realize what Jesus did when he used His choice of free will.

Free will, given by God, is our ability or power to decide from freedom of choice. With this free will we can behave in various circumstances freely of physical, public, or divine restrictions. Because of free will, we feel less moral liability for whatever the outcome might be. Because of free will, we will have positive life outcomes because we will oversee our decisions. They can achieve happiness and professional success and work better in their jobs. Contrary to the widely held belief, free will does not relieve us from our moral responsibility. We still must own up to the good things we do and the terrible things. We will not be able to blame others for our choices over which we have no control. The problem with free will is that all intentions, whether in the past, present, or future, are right or wrong. We never consider it suitable for others or right for God. We want it to be ideal for us. Our choices are not predetermined, but God already knows what choices we will make. We are still determining what will come because of our choices ahead of time. Jesus used His free will to save man. He did not have to, but it was His decision. Jesus chose to undergo these things such as agony, the whippings and thrashings, and the punishment and torture. Why do I feel convicted? It is because I know I have never been beaten like Jesus. I have never had anyone spit on me or mock me like they did to Jesus. I have never been persecuted nor suffered like Jesus. And I have never been crucified for Jesus.

It comes down to the fact that since I cannot experience what he went through, then I must commit to Jesus. But how far am I willing to follow Jesus? Often, I think about admitting defeat because it gets complicated, unpleasant, and painful.

Then, I reflect on all the things God has brought me through, and I am utterly convinced that I must be "all in!" I cannot straddle the fence or perform my duties lukewarmly. I believe in God, then I will live according to my belief. This means that when things that Jesus faces come my way, I must be willing to suffer as Christ did.

Jesus called us to a disciple's life. We must embrace that life and be willing to go where God leads us, not where we want to go. So, I asked this question again: How far am I willing to follow Jesus? My answer is to no end because I trust the path God has me on and I a nurtured in His grace!

ABOUT THE AUTHOR

Tyke Clark is originally from Florida. Born to Felton Cooper and Janie M. Clark, He grew up in a small community known as Hinson Heights. Tyke is the husband of Kimberly LaCynthia Bush-Clark. They have three daughters, Paige, Engress, and Raven. After graduating High School, Tyke served his country in the military for over 22 years. After his retirement, he continued to serve his country working for the Federal Government, both for the Department of Defense and the Department of Agriculture. Tyke has a Master's Degree in Theology, a Bachelor's Degree in Church Ministry, and an Associate Degree in Christian Studies. Tyke has volunteered in several churches during his Christian Walk and has served in positions of Elder and Deacon, Missions Committee member, member of the choir, and other various duties. He continues to serve his community by volunteering to support the Gideon International Organization and Food Shelf Organization.

DEDICATION

Thank you to Father God, who is the creator of everything, including myself. Thank you to Jesus, my Lord, and Savior, who saw my state of being and gave up His life for my own. Thank you to the Holy Spirit, who continues to serve as a guide for my daily life and keeps me on a path of peace, joy, and love.

So thankful for my daughters, Paige, Engress, and Raven who continue to inspire me with their aspirations in life and their willingness to press forward through the many challenges they face. May God keep His hands upon them in all that they pursue.

I am so grateful for my wife of nearly 40 years, who has stuck by my side through so many challenges we have had together. She has exemplified hanging in there with me through the worst, the sickest, and through extreme despondency.

Thank you to all my siblings, who, through many family challenges, continue to find ways to overcome those challenges and maintain a special love for each other and support! Special thanks to my brother and sister-in-law who also has impacted my life wonderfully and magnificently.

And I thank God for my special friends, Cornelius, Derrick, Duke, Ann, Betsy, Bob, Chris, Christie, Claudette, Karen, Lynn, Lidia, Mary, Jennifer, Robin, Rhonda, Sandy, Sherry,

Veronica, Yolanda, and many others.

And finally, thank God for my mother and mother-in-law who certainly lived out and displayed that "agape" love to their children. The women who made the most sacrifice for the best benefit and welfare of their families.

These writings come as a count of some of the many experiences that I have had in my life and where I was able to see God in those experiences. Much was revealed about what God wanted me to know about Him and what God wanted me to know about myself. I hope that as everyone reads these accounts, they allow them to pierce their hearts, minds, and souls and allow a significant change to take place within them.

I discovered my shortcomings, and I faced my lack of faith. Yet, through the hard experiences in life, God was able to break down who I was and change me into who He wanted me to be. I hope your experience will be the same.

Thank you to the many people I met, who have different personalities, and attitudes about life. It was through my different experiences with you, that I was able to learn so much, about the importance of grace!

USE TRANSLATIONS FROM THE FOLLOWING BIBLES:

Amplified Version (AMP)
English Standard Version (ESV)
Expanded Bible (EXB)
New King James Version (NKJV)
Living Bible (TLB)
The Message Bible (MSG)
New Living Translation (NLT)

MY PERSONAL TESTIMONY

SURVIVING THE NIGHT

"My faith didn't remove the pain, but it got me through the pain. Trusting God didn't diminish or vanquish the anguish, but it enabled me to endure it." - Robert Rogers

Incredibly, one statement is as true today as when the world was first created. The older you get, the more tests you go through and the more testimonies you end up having. At my current age, I have many testimonies of where God has brought me through many things, including my periods of suffering. This is one of those testimonies.

I served in the First Baptist Church as an Elder, a member of the Missions Committee, a Sound Technician, and an Approved Workman Are Not Ashamed (AWANA) Program Assistant. At that time, I was responsible for assisting the leader in guiding children from one area of the Church to another part of the church to ensure the children were receiving the appropriate training/education that was outlined in the curriculum.

But on this night, it was exceptional. It was our Grand Prix night. Children are often excited to participate in this event as they get an opportunity to build a car for the Grand Prix races that will take place. On this night, everyone was having fun, and it was exciting to watch the cars race down the track. Everyone looked intense as the cars crossed the finish line. It turned out to be a fun-filled evening. After AWANA was over, I departed and went home. In record time, I was in bed getting rest for the next day.

The following day, I woke up with a backache. It hurt enough that I texted my supervisor and informed her about my back and that I would come in to work late. About a couple of hours later, I woke up and was nauseated. My back was hurting even worse. I had to run to the bathroom because I had the urge to throw up, which I did. When I came out of the bathroom, I told my wife, Kim, I believed I needed to go to the hospital. She immediately jumped out of bed and ran to the bathroom to shower and get herself ready. While she was in the bathroom, I was bent across the sofa, trying to alleviate the pain in my back. All I knew at that time was I was in so much pain that I wanted to cry.

After Kim had gotten ready, we made our way to the car. Getting in the car, I immediately leaned back so I could be comfortable, as the pain was so excruciating. It was winter season, and at every stop Kim made, I wanted to jump out of the car and wallow in the snow, hoping it would cool the burning sensation that I had going on inside.

After arriving at the hospital and getting checked in, it wasn't long before the Emergency Staff got me checked into a room. Although I was in a lot of pain, the staff could not give me any pain medicine until they were able to identify what was causing the discomfort. I was rolled down to X-ray to have some pictures taken and then returned to the room. After my return, they gave me some medicine for the pain.

Once the doctor received the pictures of the X-rays, he came to me and explained that I had a kidney stone about the size of a golf ball, and it was stuck in my ureter. Therefore, they were going to have to operate. He explained to me that they were going to have to blast the stone into smaller pieces and place a stint in the ureter so that the small pieces would be able to flow through as I urinated. It was great to know what the problem was and know that they had a solution for the situation.

Once I was rolled in for surgery, you go through the standard procedure. Count backward from 100 until you fall asleep. It only seemed like minutes before I was awakened and found myself in the Intensive Care Unit. I was dying, as the nurse explained to me that my organs, every one of them, were shutting down. I heard someone say to contact my wife as she did not know what was going on. When Kim entered the room, she said she looked at me and knew I was not coming back.

I watched how darkness started to surround me, but there was no fear. I did not know what was to come, but it was here. Unexpectedly, I was heading to the other side. Before darkness finally closed in on me, my life flashed before my eyes, and I realized I had done much for myself but very little for God. It was too late to ask for a second chance.

And it was over. I was somewhere, but I needed to find out where I was. I tried to open my eyes but was unable to. All I knew was I was in the most serene and peaceful state that I had ever experienced in my life, and I could have stayed. I felt no pain in my body at all.

I could not tell you how long I was gone, or out, but I did

wake up, and my body was in so much pain. It was about in the early morning hours. I lay there, strapped down, with tubes running into my body.

I could barely speak, but I had to urinate badly! So, I pressed the call button, and a nurse came in. I murmured that I had to pee. The nurse left and returned with one of those jugs that a person could pee in. As I relieved myself, I saw the receptacle fill up with blood. Much blood! I thought to myself, I have never seen so much blood before.

As morning came, to my surprise, I had survived the night to a point where they felt I could be moved to another room. God was amazing! One moment, I was fighting for my life, and the next, it was like the storm was over. The crew that worked on me the night before thought I had passed until they found out I had been moved to another room and I was doing well.

After a couple of days, I was released to go home, but only for a few days. I would have to return to have the procedure for the removal of the stone. Since they had to stop the original method of removing the stone to focus on saving my life, they left everything in place except for placing a stint in the ureter. This would allow me to urinate with pain, and it was very painful using the bathroom for those few days.

Returning to the hospital on that Friday for the procedure to remove the stone, all went well.

Blasting of the stone worked, however, I still experienced painful visits to the bathroom as I urinated watching water, blood, and pieces of the stone being dispensed. That experience lasted for two about weeks.

I eventually recovered from the surgery, but I still was not out of the woods yet. But that is another testimony.

So, I must thank God for surviving this experience. It was a short road back, or so I thought. It was still early in the year, and so were many of my medical problems waiting to surface.

Now, I have a better understanding of when doctors say, if a person can survive the night, they have a better opportunity of overcoming the attack on their body.

For a moment, I wasn't there, and in an instant, I was back! And although I was out for hours, it seemed like only seconds to me. Maybe it was an experience of living outside of time itself. But it was a great experience.

To God be the glory, forever and always! He showed me how quickly He can take life and how quickly He can restore it.

I now know absolutely nothing happens without God's approval. And sometimes it doesn't have anything to do with our sin, it has to do with God's permission and the involvement of His own hands. Learning from Job taught me a lot, but going through this experience taught me even more!

I will never take life for granted again. Amen!

Isaiah 45:4-8 "For the sake of Jacob My servant, And of Israel My chosen, I have also called you by your name; I have given you an honorable name though you have not known Me. "I am the LORD, and there is no one else; There is no God except Me. I will embrace and arm you, though you have not known Me, that people may know from the rising to the setting of the sun, the world over. That there is no one except Me. I am the LORD, and there is no other, the One forming light and creating darkness, causing peace and creating disaster; I am the LORD who does all these things. "Rain down, O heavens, from above, let the clouds pour down righteousness, all the blessings of God; let the earth open up, let salvation bear fruit, and righteousness spring up with it; I, the LORD, have created it.

Doing it My Way
(Patience)

"Trying to get through life on your own limited strength, knowledge, and resources leads to futility and a loss of hope. But in God's economy, getting to the end of yourself is the beginning of hope." – Henry Cloud

Judges 17:6 "In those days, there was no king in Israel, but every man did what was right in his own eyes."

In 1969, Frank Sinatra wrote a song where the lyrics began this way: "And now the end is near, and as I face the final curtain. My friend, I will say it. Clearly, I'll state my case, of which I am certain. I've lived a full life. I've traveled on every highway. But more, much more than this. I did it my way...."

You know, I have always been transparent about myself. And I am going to be even more obvious. Although I didn't hear the song until much later in life, I LOVED that song! I still long for the song. But I am older now and much more mature.

If there is any song that was ever written and a song that pointed people away from Christ, it is this one. The words I, I'll, I'm, I've, and I were mentioned at least 30 times or more in the song.

And then another set of lyrics says: "For what is a man what has he got. If not himself, then he is naught. To say what he feels and not the words of one who kneels." This certainly blows me away!

I am not here to accuse anyone who may listen to secular music. I will not even judge secular music. But if the circular song points me away from Christ and causes me to look more at myself, I must reevaluate that song.

I can do nothing on my own outside of Christ. Any achievements, accomplishments, attainments, promotions, successes, or wins come by the hand of God. And if the songs I listen to point me from praising God to praising myself, I have seriously derailed.

I must be careful of the millions of songs like these. They make me think less of God and more of myself. They are friendly and beautiful, yet they can be deceitful and cause me to become self-centered.

As a believer, I should follow the rules that do not cause me to reject God. It's not always about my rights but about God's righteousness.

As part of any ministry and running any programs, I must always endeavor and ensure that whatever I do, in my creativity, I do not violate the policies of God's command and man's law. Though we have many members, we are still one body. And the body does not operate against itself. So, I don't do it my way; we do it together, in unison, with unity, and with uniformity for the glory of God!

Prayer: Father God, sometimes we have leaders appointed over us, but we do not feel appropriately led. So, we sometimes follow the established rules and do what is right with our own eyes. A lack of leadership sometimes affects the wisdom you have bestowed upon us. Please help us represent You in the holiest ways, regardless of who is in charge. It is in Your name we pray, amen!

Getting the Credit or Facing the Consequences (Obedience)

"All men make mistakes, but a good man yields when he knows his course is wrong and repairs the evil. The only crime is pride." – Sophocles, Antigone.

James 4:17 "So whoever knows the right thing to do and does not do it is a sin for him."

I can make bad decisions. How do I keep credibility after making an unwise decision? I confess that I made the decision. A mistaken judgment may only affect us for the moment, or it could hang around with us for the rest of our lives. It could cost us our family, friends, or even our jobs. Is the risk too much to take? If I make bad decisions, I will face the consequences!

However, I could seek the wisdom of the Holy Spirit to help me make good decisions. A servant who makes good decisions selects actions that provide the most excellent result for God and others. A wise person makes decisions with an open mind and does not allow their predispositions to affect them. They are rational in their decision after gaining knowledge and understanding from God.

Our last foundation of accountability is credit or consequences. We prove accountability when we know we will directly take the bow or take liability for the outcome of our endeavors.

Prayer: Father God, forgive me because I am so full of my elaborate self. Having this self-importance indicates I certainly have evil in my heart. I know the right thing to do and choose not to do it. I am a sinful creature who genuinely needs You. So, please help me always to have You in mind, which will help me always to do the right thing. It is in Your magnificent name I pray, amen!

I Want to Obey
(Obedience; Patience)

"If worship does not propel us into greater obedience, it has not been worship. To stand before the Holy One of eternity is to change." – Richard J. Foster.

In Matthew 10:34–39, Jesus stated what it means to follows Him. He said, "Do not suppose that I have come to bring peace to the earth. I did not come to bring peace but a sword. For I have come to turn a man against his father, a daughter against her mother, a daughter-in-law against her mother-in-law—a man's enemies will be the members of his own household.' Anyone who loves their father or mother more than me is not worthy of me; anyone who loves their son or daughter is not worthy of me. Whoever does not take up their cross and follow me is not worthy of me. Whoever finds their life will lose it, and whoever loses their life for my sake will find it."

What does "follow Jesus" mean? We come up with our responses to answer this question. But, in a nutshell, following Christ means striving to be like Him.

So, what is my struggle? Well, I may need clarification on Paul's words. Paul asked us to imitate him as he imitates Christ (1 Cor 11:1). This is what Paul wanted us to do when he did the right thing. However, Paul reminded us that he becomes conflicted in serving God. Paul said that he did not do what he wanted for the good, but Paul practiced the evil that he did not wish to do (Rom 7:19). Paul said he found himself doing the things he shouldn't and not doing the things that he should be doing. This is where most of us find ourselves. We intend to do things the way God called us to do it. But we have difficulty choosing what God will have us do over what we feel like doing.

Paul did not stop there either. He continues to point out the weakness that we all share. Paul wrote, "It is no longer I who does it, but it is a sin living in me" (Romans 7:17). As Christians, we are trying to live a righteous life, but the spiritual battle is a tough battle to be in. What makes it so difficult? It is not always the enemy. Sometimes, it's those closest to us that make choosing God's righteousness over our self-righteousness. Sometimes, our roadblocks are family members, longtime friends, awesome neighbors, and great colleagues. This puts weight on the choices we need to make to honor God.

What can I do about this to help me overcome these challenges of choosing to follow God? I can begin by checking my mindset. Many things often need to be corrected when I react based on my feelings rather than accurate and factual information. The way I feel is unpredictable, sometimes dishonest, and often unwise. My feelings are a gift, but I must let the Spirit of God control them.

If I choose obedience to God, then it pleases God. God's love inspires us to obey Him. Yet, I can still fall short. Jesus stated if I love Him, I will keep His commandments. If I live for God, I will practice correct behavior.

I ask God to examine my heart. I even asked Him to create in me a clean soul. Creating a clean one will require work because God may examine my heart. If I am unwilling to surrender to God's will, I will not be compliant, supportive, or open to God and His commands. God wants a servant who has a heart for obeying.

Let's give God some glory by our obedience. There is a definite correlation between my obedience and God's credit. As I study our Bible, I see that when the people obeyed God, His glory shined exceedingly bright. I refer to the sanctuary and the Tabernacle building and see a clear example. So, do I want God to have His glory?

If I can pledge to be submissive to God, no matter what, my spirit will unite with the Holy Spirit. And the Holy Spirit will encourage me to comply with the Lord despite my conflicting emotions.

To follow Jesus, I must always obey God and try to do the right thing. When I follow Jesus, I indeed let Him be the Supervisor. I am not saved by my work for Jesus but by what He did for me. He gave me His grace, and I want to please Him. This means following His examples when confronted with many of today's challenges. If I allow the Holy Spirit to control my life, I will please Jesus.

Following Jesus means applying God's truths, learning from His Word, and living as if Jesus were walking alongside me.

God has told me what He requires of me and given me the power to do it. God gave me His Spirit. Do we remember Augustine's prayer, "O Lord, command what you will, and give what you command?" So, when God tells us what He wants us to do, He also gives us the power to do it! We need to be steadfast in keeping God's statutes.

Prayer: Jesus, our Lord, and Savior. We certainly need you in this area of our life. It is so hard to obey when obedience is called for. Please help us to follow You, Your ways, and Your example. Please help me to exemplify Your righteousness before others. Amen!

Remaining Calm During the Storm (Patience; Faith)

"Worry does not empty tomorrow of its sorrows. It empties today of its strength." – Corrie Ten Boom

Colossians 1:17, And He Himself existed and is before all things, and in Him all things hold together. His is the controlling, cohesive force of the universe.

Matthew 8:23-27 talks about the disciples facing an awful storm. This occurred as the disciples and Jesus crossed the Sea of Galilee in a boat.

Unexpectedly, a great storm developed. The disciples became afraid; even though Jesus was with them, they still became worried. These are the men that Jesus picked with His own hands, yet they were concerned. Although this was an actual storm, it was a turbulent time. Didn't Jesus give the disciples standards to follow in times of trouble? So, what happened with their faith when the storm came?

None of us, believers and non-believers, are exempt from the storms of life. Even though I may have great faith, I don't know how I will respond in times of distress. Les Brown, a motivational speaker, said, "Adversity introduces a man to himself." How we react during times of hardship reveals how much faith we have in God.

I already know many things run through my mind that would test my faith. The loss of my wife or one of my children, being displaced from my home, loss of financial support, severe illnesses, etc. Until we have been placed on this path, where the storm is directly in front of us, we have no idea how we will respond until the storm hits. Remember Peter? What damage will have occurred once the storm leaves? The home I once had is now an empty lot. The brand-new car I just purchased is a total wreck. I once had money, I thought I was set for life, but I could be on the sidewalk begging for handouts. These are the natural storms of people, but my response to the storm dictates how God helps us.

There is no shame in feeling fear. But God said if I am afraid, He did not give me that fear. I look at what happens in my life; things can impact me so much that they weaken my faith. God gave me something fabulous to counteract my anxieties at certain moments: a great spirit. This spirit gives me strength, love, and a wise mind.

So, how does one remain calm when a storm is happening? Jesus said He gave us everything we need to have peace during our times of trouble and sorrow, but we must be courageous (John 16:33).

Jesus warned us that we would experience every kind of pressure, not just some pressure, but every kind, from all sides. We are instructed to stay in the fight and not quit because quitting is not an option. We will face persecution as a believer, but we must remember that we knew this before we signed up. And we must remember God is with us (2 Corinthians 4:8-9).

Seasons will change in our lives. We will have sunshine and rain, heat and shade. We will win and lose in this life. We have heard it said many times: either we enter a storm, live in it, or come out of it. No matter where we are, we must seek God because He will deliver us from all our worries.

Prayer: Father of the Universe, sometimes there is so much chaos in our lives that we do not know how to handle the situations. We fret over things we cannot control and are at a loss as to what steps to take to help us. We pray that You calm our spirit during these times and help us realize our trust and confidence are in You. Amen!

Thinking About Other Things
(Patience; Thoughtfulness)

"What you are determines the world in which you live, so as you change, your world changes also." — Norman Vincent Peale

Philippians 4:8 "Finally, brothers, whatever is true, whatever is honorable, whatever is, whatever is pure, whatever is lovely, whatever is commendable, if there is any excellence, if there is anything worthy of praise, think about these things."

I love to have peace in my life. I invested in self-help books and programs and met with others to bring peace. But these things only brought temporary peace to me because what I was investing in was not perfected.

To achieve perfect peace, I needed to start with trusting God. I say I trust God, but I often felt like I must do something in the natural because I did not understand how God worked in the supernatural. Here is my saying, "if Tye is thinking it, then God is not!" In Isaiah 55:8-9, God teaches us that our thoughts and ways are not His. God says, "As high as the heavens are above the earth, so are My ways higher than yours." This makes knowing the essence of who God is very hard for us.

However, God has given me instructions on achieving perfect peace in Him. He told me to always keep my mind on Him. One would have thought that if I trusted him, I could keep my mind on Him (Isaiah 26:3). He also gave me some specific things to place in my mind and focus on. I needed to think about ethical and dishonest, transparent and lucid, beautiful, praiseworthy and admirable, and what is virtuous and pure. But my mind was always on improper, questionable, unreasonable, disgusting, wrong and shameful, and wicked and sinful things. This is quite a task God has required me when I am inundated with thoughts of failure, dishonesty, irresponsibility, homeliness, and imperfection.

Prayer: Lord Jesus, we pray for excellence in You. So, please help us be trustworthy and honorable. Whether others are in our presence or not, we will respect them. Please help us be pure, wholesome, and lovely. Use us to be peace bearers. Let us praise You and keep our mind, soul, spirit, and heart centered on You.

The Sweet of the Fruit (Kindness)

"Good thoughts bear good fruit, bad thoughts bear bad fruit."
— James Allen

Galatians 5:16 "But I say, walk by the Spirit, and you will not gratify the desires of the flesh."

Why is the Fruit of the Spirit sweet? The Fruit of the Spirit represents God's traits, and if we remember Psalm 34, it tells us to taste and see that the Lord is good! Can I end this writing right now?

I had to take a moment to see why these traits are essential to God. Love is a feeling for me, but love is a choice for God. I decided to love others and make a sacrifice of myself for the sake of those I love. Jesus is the ideal example of love. He chose to love me through His death, even though I am a sinner. (Rom. 5:8). Jesus gave Himself for me and everyone else. I give of myself only for the ones I love. I now recognize the difference between my love and having the love of Jesus!

Joy is pleasure and cheerfulness despite how things are going in our lives. Jesus made it possible to share His joy (John 15:11). James 1:2 told me that when I am being evaluated and facing all kinds of trials, I should count it as joy. This is because my faith is being tested, and my perseverance has increased. I often interchange happiness and joy, but happiness changes and depends on my external conditions. Still, joy relies only on God, who never changes.

I needed to distinguish between world peace and the Peace of God. World peace is conditional and is based on my internal feelings at the time. I only have Peace if I can see it with my natural eyes. There is no room for any difficulties. I always felt I must manage the situation. I try to be in control, and it will eventually stop.

Jesus says in John 14:27, "Peace I leave with you; my Peace, I give you. I do not give to you as the world gives..." This Peace depends on trust and does not have to be seen with the naked eye. It does not matter if trouble comes our way; we can still have God's Peace in our lives. We do not have to worry about managing the situation because we know God is in control. This is everlasting. We can enjoy this Peace of God because we are no longer at war with Him.

One thing I am not is slow to get angry! If I was, then I would undoubtedly possess long-suffering. I would show great self-restraint during my times of frustration. I would not always rush to quickly get revenge or chastise those I felt wronged me. As a believer in God's Word, I should show tolerance and mercy to those who provoke, dispute, or think of me in harmful ways. If God holds back His anger from me, shouldn't I do the same towards others (2 Peter 3:9).

Gentleness requires me to be kind to others even if they do not deserve it. God is kind to me through His grace. I do not deserve compassion from God, but He gave it to me anyway

(Tit. 3:7; Eph. 2:7; Rom. 2:4). I continue to learn I must wear "kindness" all the time (Col. 3:12). This is a real dilemma for me.

One would see gentleness and goodness as the same thing, but not in the eyes of God. God is good (Psalm 100:5; 34:8), and Jesus is God. And we are to imitate Jesus. When we imitate Jesus, we reflect the goodness of our God. The Bible has stated twice that "goodness" is the fruit of the Spirit (Gal. 5:22 and Eph. 5:9). Isn't this enough to say we must practice it? I know it sounds crazy, but we do not repay evil with evil, but we repay evil with good (Romans 12:17- 21; Matthew 5:44; 1 Pet. 3:9- 11).

Here is why God loves people with faith in Him (Gal 5:6). A faithful person is reliable and responsible.

This person can be trustworthy. God can have "Confidence"; this person will not let Him down. God knows that when this person gives their word, they will do what they said. This person is steadfast. Hmmmm. Will I ever get there?

Meekness is misunderstood as a weakness. Men believe meekness is flawed in Spirit and bravery and lacks courage. God views meekness as power under control. In other words, our passions must be controlled. Happy is the believer who lets God have control. I learned I had to stop going in my obstinate ways and battling in opposition to God! I may have the form of looking weak, but I could be a lion in God's eyes. (Matt. 5:5, Psalm 25:9). I admit I am not firm in defending myself, but I give my defense to God and His truth.

Do I need temperance? Absolutely! As a believer, my eyes should be on the goal of winning Christ's approval (Phil. 3:8).

I should allow the power and control of the Holy Spirit to take over. I must do away with everything that impedes the achievement of that goal. My flesh is useless when I allow the Holy Spirit to take control (Gal. 5:19-21, Eph. 5:18). If I walk in the Spirit, I need to ignore the desires of my flesh (Gal. 5:16).

So why is the Fruit of the Spirit sweet to me? It cultivates my heart and encourages me to live by the Spirit. And if I live by the Spirit, my heart leans toward God. I will no longer worry about what the world assumes about me. I only care about pressing forward to become more like God.

Prayer: Lord Jesus, please help us because our flesh and Spirit are constantly fighting. If they agree on anything, we never notice it. Help us to chase after the ways of the Spirit because we know it is always representing You, and if we remain in company with the Spirit, we will stay in company with You, amen!

Living Within God's Grace
(Grace, Peace)

"Your worst days are never so bad that you are beyond the reach of God's grace. And your best days are never so good that you are beyond the need of God's grace." – Jerry Bridges

Psalm 86:15 "But you, O Lord, are a God merciful and gracious, slow to anger and abounding in steadfast love and faithfulness."

God extends grace to me daily, but it is difficult for me to do the same for others. I have salvation in Jesus and know I am headed somewhere lovely after leaving Earth. But my lifeline has so much to do with the grace of God. I know that people would die by the billions daily if not for God's grace. We would not worry about overpopulation, but moreover, underpopulation.

I learn that God loves me and shows me daily through His merciful grace. I cannot recognize when God's grace prevails during my worst days. But, looking back, I see His whole presence.

The Bible tells me God's incredible and unearned grace brought redemption and deliverance to all men. God's grace teaches me to discard ungodliness and immoral requests. It teaches me to live practical, decent, and devout lives. My life has a purpose that should replicate a mature spiritual Christian. Those of us who have lived long enough because of God's grace predict and assuredly expect the splendid appearance of God and Jesus Christ.

Christ eagerly gave Himself to be oppressed, tortured, and crucified to free me from all malice, mischief, and evil. Jesus's death purified us because He chose me for Himself (Matthew 16:24-25). After all, I am incredibly special to Him. Because of Jesus's sacrifice, I should be enthusiastic about doing good for others and extending that grace to others, as God has repeatedly extended it to me.

Grace helps me do what I could never do on my own. God told Paul, "My grace is sufficient for you," God gave Paul the power to be set free from the aggravation crushing him.

Grace has given me a life not condemned by God. I am forgiven for altering my belief. This belief results in my mind and heart being renewed. Because of grace, I will have a life God wants me to have.

So why am I having this talk about grace? God gives it to me daily, and I forget about it daily. Here is how God knows I forget about it. Grace means forgiveness of an offense. It means help and power to triumph over all the sins God shows me. Grace means taking the time to work on my salvation, as Jesus instructed.

If I experience the Grace of God, then I certainly have God's favor in my life. I will control my tongue, actions, and emotions as a believer. I will be polite and pleasant, even when I am not in the presence of others. While walking in this world, grace has shown me how to carry myself as others will see me play the role of being a child of God through my actions.

Prayer: Father God, we beg for forgiveness every day because we constantly forget about the grace You give to us. Please help us recognize Your grace during our time of distress. And help us, especially when our lives are at peace, that You are with us even more. Amen!

Discounting the Acts of Those Who Hurt Us (Forgiveness; Love)

"Anger, resentment and jealousy doesn't change the heart of others - it only changes yours." – Shannon Alder

1 Corinthians 13:5b "Love isn't selfish or quick-tempered. It doesn't keep a record of wrongs that others do."

I wish I had a heart like God! A heart willing to forgive no matter how often a person offends me. It is much harder for me to forgive others when they offend me. To become an expert, I would require a lot of practice. The tradeoff is that I will often be offended as I grow stronger in forgiving others.

I am not saying the tradeoff is fair, but it is beneficial. Proverbs 19:11 says that good sense makes one slow to anger, and it is His glory to overlook an offense.

If I can overlook an offense, it indicates I am growing in a gospel emotional response. I can also enjoy genuine praise. If I have a short fuse for anger, anything people say or do will offend me. But if I use the gospel sense, people will believe I understand well. Think about it this way. The more I allow the gospel's truth to renew my attitude and shape my viewpoints, the easier I will look past offenses.

If I own up to my sins, I can rejoice in overlooking those who offend me. In the book of Matthew, I am reminded that if I remove the plank from my own eyes, I can see more clearly. The most joyful believers are those who repent the quickest. These believers are faster at owning up to their wrongdoings. They quickly humble themselves and "chill out" in Jesus. As God's Word moves us from the criticism of the devil and into the conviction of the Holy Spirit, we adhere to the fact that we need God's grace as much as anyone else who sins.

If I can overlook an offense, I know God's grace and Spirit are becoming more practical, changing my life. As a believer, I should grow in the grace and knowledge of Jesus Christ (2 Peter 3:18). As I accomplish this, I am getting to know Jesus better. And if I give in to the work of the Holy Spirit, He will grow His fruits within me. These fruits are love, joy, peace, patience, kindness, goodness, faithfulness, gentleness, and self-control (Galatians 5:22-23).

If I can overlook an offense, I can gain freedom. I should be someone whose joy is not connected to what others think and say about me, nor how they relate and react to me (Proverbs 29:25). Fearing people doesn't always mean I am afraid of them. Still, I rely too much on their approval. Who is fueling my joy, God or man?

If I can overlook an offense, I know I am getting better at forgiving those who offend me, just like Jesus forgave me and continues to forgive me. I can imagine that all my sins—every sinful thought, word, and deed—are forgiven by Christ. Is it correct that I withhold my forgiveness from others (Matthew 18:21-35)?

God's compassion led me to repentance (Romans 2:4). So,

what do I think my unyielding feelings, easily offended, and record keeping of the wrongs of other attitudes will lead people? It is best to follow Paul's simple instructions. We must be kind to one another, sympathetic, and understanding one another, as God in Christ displayed those same traits toward us (Ephesians 4:32).

To help me forgive myself, I need to start by accepting that someone hurt me. I must pray for sincere regard before seeking counsel from others. I must pray for my own heartbroken Spirit and the Spirit of the other person. And as hard as it will be, I must walk through forgiveness even when I don't feel like it. This means I must act graciously towards the person who offended me. When I do so, I will heal much more quickly.

According to Proverb 29:11, if I am a sensible person, I will control my temper and earn the respect of the offender by overlooking their wrongdoings.

Prayer: Jesus, my Lord! You have demonstrated what it means to forgive others. But teach us to forgive others through simple actions and words, letting others know that we have forgiven them and are ready to move forward. And help us overcome the pain as we move towards love. It is in Your name we pray, amen!

God's Provision for My Needs (Generosity)

"When you eagerly depend upon the Lord for any provision, you eliminate all odds of disappointment." – Gift Gugu Mona

Genesis 22:14 So Abraham called the name of that place, "The Lord will provide"; as it is said to this day, "On the mount of the Lord it shall be provided."

Before coming to Minnesota, we (my family) resided in Hawaii for five years. The experience was different from what I expected. Before coming to Hawaii, we were in Korea for nine years. I was looking forward to retirement. Even at one-half the pay, we would be okay. Not extravagant living, but okay.

When we arrived in Hawaii, I was shocked at the cost of living. Incredibly, anyone can live there. Most people live there because of the weather. It never changes, or at best, it ranges from 10 to 20 degrees, but it never really gets below 50 degrees, which is considered freezing.

With my retirement check, I expected to take half of my pension, pay for somewhere to stay, and use the other part to pay for utilities and other minor expenses. Instead, the house we rented took my entire retirement check. The job I had spent well, but the utilities, groceries, and other expenses consumed that paycheck. More investment is needed in savings. That was living from paycheck to paycheck.

Believe it or not, my wife Kim and I could not go out and do any extracurricular activities or even go to a movie during that first year because the money was not there. I later discovered that two and three generations lived in one house because it was the only way to survive.

We were a working family of four, with one car to transport us to all our different destinations during the workweek. Kim served as the taxi driver for all of us. Her day started early in the morning, taking us, one at a time, to our various destinations. By the time she dropped off the last person, it was nearly time for her to start picking us up.

After some time, and through all the grumbling and complaining I did, I could look back and reflect on our survival for that first year. I had to give God His due glory!!!

Yes, we were a family with one car, but that one car took everyone everywhere they were supposed to go. And yes, I did not make a penny extra than I needed to, but all the bills got paid, and we had food to eat and clothes to wear. God provided shelter and the necessities of life. But I was blinded by what I wanted my life to be like more than what it was.

Acknowledging God and giving Him thanks for all He had done led to us acquiring a second car and then a third car. Sometimes, God wants us to see Him in our "tight" situations and acknowledge who He is and what He does. Unfortunately, we do not see that unless we use hindsight.

Prayer: My Father, You provide for us daily, yet sometimes we fail to see it. Our eyes are primarily on what we don't have, not what we have. Please help us realize we only need what's required for today, not tomorrow or next year. Please help us remember Your Word, which says give us our daily bread. Provide us only what we need today. It is in Your name, we pray, amen!

Having A Heart Like God
(Gentleness)

"No beauty shines brighter than that of a good heart." –
Shanina Shaik

Galatians 2:20 "I have been crucified with Christ. No longer I
live, but Christ who lives in me. And the life I now live in the
flesh, I live by faith in the Son of God, who loved and gave
himself for me."

I can still remember when I was a kid and saw someone
famous; I told myself I wanted to be just like that person.
I made that statement without knowing where the person
was from, who that person was, and what they had gone
through to become who they were. I remember watching
Bishop Thomas Dexter Jakes (Renowned Pastor.) In an
interview, Bishop Jakes mentioned encountering a young
man who said, "You got it made! I would love to have what
you have." Bishop Jakes responded, "Are you willing to go
through what I went through to get what I have?"

I pray often, and in our prayer, I pray to have a heart just
like God. We know that God is a god that has agape love for
His people. The Bible describes King David as a man after
God's heart (1 Sam 13:14). Yet David was very sinful (2 Sam
11), but God showered David with His love. To have a heart

like God requires me to be unchanging in my love towards others. How do I achieve this? It involves a transformation of my mind; I must become filled with the Holy Spirit; I should spend time alone with God; and I must be obedient even in the most minor of requests from God.

Consequently, can I have a heart like God? Can I face disappointments, endure heartbreaks, suffer through rejection, bear abandonment, overlook mocking, and still have a forgiving heart towards those who oppress me? Can I do it for the sake of the Gospel so I can have that heart like God?

God's heart is broken daily, yet He does not withhold grace from our lives. God's agape love ensures grace prevails, regardless of how often we sin and rebel against Him.

Prayer: Father, please have patience with us as we develop a heart like Yours. So much of what is required is complex, and the struggle to be kind and forgive others is difficult. But You are faithful, and we will trust You for this transformation of our hearts. It is in Jesus' name we pray, amen!

Letting the Goodness of the God's Light Shine Through Us (Self-Control)

"Don't fight darkness- bring the light, and darkness will disappear." – Maharishi Mahesh Yogi

Ephesians 5:9 "For the fruit of light is found in all that is good and right and true."

One of the fruits of the Spirit is self-control. We are all prone to losing control of ourselves, from time to time. I know that I have in my life. And when I did lose control, I found myself going back to that individual and apologizing either for my words or my actions.

Why do I lose self-control? Why do I let things consume my life? I have found that when I experience the contributing factors of anger, resentment, fear, concern, stress, pressure, anxiety, and grief, I get angry. Learning to lean on the Holy Spirit to help me realize when these emotions are beginning to escalate has turned out to be a big plus for me. The calming voice of the Spirit helps my flesh of irrationality submit to the Spirit of Reasoning.

If we do good, act good, and display good for the sake of the

Lord, then the fruit of the light is in us. God said let our lights so shine that others will see our good deeds and glorify Him. So, let us ensure we are practicing doing good for God and the sake of the Gospel.

Prayer: Lord Jesus, Your bright light makes our way transparent, so we should not stumble around. Please help us get on with it when it's time to be more affectionate and caring than antagonistic and unsympathetic! Help us see that decency, morality, and truth are appropriate for our daylight hours. Help us determine what will please You and encourage us to do it. Amen!

Learning to Communicate Through Grace
(Grace, Kindness)

"Any problem, big or small, within a family always seems to start with bad communication. Someone is not listening." – Emma Thompson

Philippians 2:4 "Let each of you look not only to his own interests but also to the interests of others."

There is no doubt that our form of communication is better than ever. We have telephones, cell phones, emailing, and texting capabilities. We can even create a video and use the Internet to host meetings. However, we need to be more connected. So why do we still need to improve our communication with others? The answer is our inability to pay attention, appreciate, convey, express truth, and cooperate.

Every day, God communicates His grace to me. He is undeniable in everything He says. There is no room for misinterpretation or miscommunication. Looking through my eyes, it should be evident that I have grace with every step and breath I take. God's grace is produced spiritually, which I experience naturally. He shares His grace through His Word, but I can't understand like He wants me to. He shares

His grace within my mind, but I can't think how He wants me to. He shares His grace through my heart, but I can't feel how He wants me to.

It should never be my place to dominate the conversation but listen to others as they speak. I would want to control the conversation because I don't want anyone else to listen to anything else that could be said in the conversation. I only want others to listen to me!

I should listen to others communicate and hear what they have to share. Grace is everything, even in communication.

Proverbs 18:2 says, "A fool does not delight in understanding but only in expressing his opinion." So, when God speaks to us, it is okay to talk back. He wants to hear out of our mouths what we feel in our hearts.

I keep this thought in my mind because I want to please my Lord! The "sacrifice of fools" gives God lip service without changing lives. If I do have something to say to God, let it be something worthwhile and not about my own opinion. I am grateful that God's grace still prevails, even with some of the language that escapes my lips.

Prayer: Father God, teach us not to push to the front. Please help us avoid sweet-talking on our way to the top. Instead, help us put ourselves aside and help others move ahead. Please help us be obsessed with giving others the advantage and allow us to forget ourselves long enough to lend a helping hand. Amen!

Forgiving Those in Need of Forgiveness (Gentleness; Forgiveness-Christmas)

"We must develop and maintain the capacity to forgive. He who is devoid of the power to forgive is devoid of the power to love," – Martin Luther King Jr.

Psalm 103:10-14 "He does not deal with us according to our sins, nor repay us according to our iniquities. As high as the heavens are above the earth, so great is His steadfast love toward those who fear Him; as far as the east is from the west, so far does He remove our transgressions from us. As a father shows compassion to his children, the Lord shows compassion to those who fear Him. For He knows our frame; He remembers that we are dust."

The Christmas season is upon us once again. We labeled it "The most wonderful time of the year!" So, why do we observe this time as delightful? This season continues to grow across the entire world. It brings something unique to those who have not believed, even amid spiritual battles.

Why is there more emphasis on fellowship around this time? Being around family and friends sometimes brings fun, laughter, happiness, and joy. It demonstrates to us our need to have those we love and care for around us. Like with our Christian brothers and sisters, this time of gathering serves as exceptional food for our souls. Evangelizing to others is excellent, but we must periodically allow ourselves to be refueled so our strength is not eaten away. Be rejuvenated during this particular time.

And why do we give gifts? Gifts around this time symbolize the honors and praises made to our Lord and Savior, Jesus Christ! The Three Wise Men started this tradition over 2000 years ago, and it continues to this day!

Through Jesus' death, the ultimate gift was given—the gift of eternal life. It wasn't placed in a box and wrapped in excellent Christmas paper. It did not have a small card with a unique message on it. It was not adorned with the most stunning bow on the box. The gift was a baby, giving up all his Kingship, Princehood, and glory for the sake of love for people who knew Him not.

Jesus is the gift that still gives. He continues to provide for those who accept Him as their King and Savior. He continuously expresses His love for strangers because everyone needs forgiveness.

As we spend this time with others this season, let us think of the strangers we encounter. As we engage in conversation with them, remember the importance of loving them and sharing Jesus' forgiveness with them. It may lead them to a promised eternal life.

We, ourselves, do not want to be devoid of love or live a life of unforgiveness. We want forgiveness in our hearts, to live a life of love like Jesus. And we want to demonstrate that love and forgiveness towards others who do not even know us.

Prayer: Father, thank You so much for the love that covers the multitude of our sins. We have seen it firsthand because our lives have been spared. You died for our iniquities, though You had none of Your own. For that, we are so grateful. So, as You remember us as people who need forgiveness from You, let us remember those who need forgiveness from us. Amen!

When God Gives, and
We Do Not Know
(Grace)

"The meaning of life is to find your gift. The purpose of life is to give it away." – Pablo Picasso

Romans 12:6 "Having gifts that differ according to the grace given to us, let us use them: if prophecy, in proportion to our faith."

When we were birthed, God did not give us life empty-handed. He blessed us with a measure of faith and with at least one gift. The trust measurement given to each of us who used these gifts is seldom displayed. Some of us spend more than half our lives trying to figure out what gifts we have.

God's word says we each received a gift (1 Peter 4:10). We are instructed to use that gift to serve each other. When we do, we fulfill our duties as good stewards of God. Our kindness towards one another is displayed in many ways. One of those ways is using our gifts to support each other.

Discovering our spiritual gifts is like shopping for a physical gift for someone. We struggle with the search because we put ourselves in a position to be up against time. Every second of our lives is precious. These seconds have given us an obtuse view of the priorities of life. The business we have invited distracts us from those closest to us. Work and commitments monopolize most of our day. How much time are we investing in discovering our gifts, and how much time do we use them after we find them?

It is good when we discover God's gift to us. We struggle because we do not know how to implement that gift. Others often know what our gifts are before we do. They observe us during times of adversity and watch our responses. They watch as we branch out without fear. Some people even manage how well we connect with God's Word and work in God's will. And they sum up all their observation by coming up to you and saying, "You have a great gift!" And when others say that to us, we respond, "Oh, that was nothing." It's because, for the gift user, it requires little effort.

Our gift is when we do the most work with the least effort. All things work for the good. God, who is excellent in us, works with our outer self to do the impossible without us thinking about it.

Why don't we recognize our gifts? It's because we can't see in ourselves what others perceive. During hard times, some of us let our best qualities come out. When times are tough, we focus on solving, not reflecting on the cause. God knows our divine potential. If we pray and ask Him about it, He will help us recognize it.

Here is one of the most remarkable things about our possession of the gift(s) God gave us. Even though we may not know what the gift(s) are, we may use the gift(s) without knowing.

God empowers everyone with a gift, which the Spirit manifests for the common good. God provides wisdom, knowledge, faith, restoration, the working of wonders, divination, the ability to differentiate between spirits, diverse kinds of tongues, and the interpretation of tongues. The Spirit distributes these gifts to each of us individually as He wills.

Some people do not believe in these gifts or think they must be updated. They don't believe that gifts work, and they find it hard to believe that God will give a gift to all people.

As followers of Christ, we must believe what the Bible says regarding faith and Christian practice. It is Holy, and it is true. We cannot accept the Bible in part, but we must believe It in whole. We must believe that God gives everyone gifts, good and bad people. But most of all, according to God's words, we must assume that these gifts are irrevocable (Romans 11:29). We can choose to use the gifts to serve God or the world. Sadly, so many have accepted the gift from the Giver and used it to serve themselves instead.

I hope we discover our gift and are not self-serving with it. I pray that we are selfless and generous in using it to serve others, as God has commanded.

Prayer: Heavenly Father, thank You for the spiritual gifts You gave to all of us. Let us not walk through life without using them. Please help us recognize them and use them to serve You and each other for the good of Your Kingdom. Amen!

Remaining Connected to God During Times of Adversity (Faith)

"Be much alone with God, and take time to get thoroughly acquainted. Converse over everything with Him. Unburden yourself wholly -every thought, feeling, wish, plan, and doubt- to Him...He wants not merely to be on good terms with you but to be intimate." – Horatius Bonar

Psalm 23:4 "Even though I walk through the valley of the shadow of death, I will fear no evil, for you are with me; your rod and your staff, they comfort me."

If ever a time we find the need for God in our life, it is during our time of loss. Those who have much and those who have little realize this is one life event everyone has in common. We will not escape the emotional turmoil that comes with the passing of a loved one.

A good support group to help us through our pain and suffering is always great! It is great to be surrounded by a group of individuals who express compassion and care for what we are experiencing and pray for us. But once the dust settles and the moments of silence begin, how do we manage our emotions and our faith? What do we do before we realize it is just God and us?

Well, David continued to seek out God. He searched for Him and thirsted for Him (Psalm 22:1-2.) Even if we begin to experience sadness, we must continue to seek sanctuary in God and pray for His strength. We need His continued love and kindness. These things are better for us than life, we must continue to praise Him and bless Him. And when we praise Him, we must do it with great joy. We must lift our hands to God in prayer. There we will be delighted.

Even as we lay awake at night, we should think of God. We must remember how much He has already helped us. We must not forget that when we were in trouble, we could rejoice through the tribulation because we remain protected beneath the shadows of His wings. And in our time of distress, we must follow close behind Him because God said He would save us with His strong right arm.

We all will face the pain of losing someone dear to us. But we must remember we will make that same journey.

Sharing with others increases our chances of connecting with the people we speak with. These people include friends, relatives, and even people we do not know. The connections we create can be meaningful and will remind us of our shared humanity. As we share, we often experience a sense of pleasure in our suffering.

As believers, God appointed us to share the assurance we have in Christ with others. As we do not know the day we will leave nor when our loved ones depart this Earth, let us never pass up the opportunity to share with others. When we share with others, we share a measure of the grace God extended to others.

Prayer: Father God, as we pray, we ask for a strong anchor in You. Especially when hardship and disappointments come our way, please allow us to be vessels of encouragement to each other when adversity strikes. We will always need your strength and your love. It is in Your name we pray, amen!

Understanding God's Grace
(A Reason to be Thankful!)
(Grace; Gratitude; Gratefulness)

"I am no longer anxious about anything, as I realize the Lord can carry out His will, and His will is mine. It makes no matter where He places me or how. That is rather for Him to consider than for me; for in the easiest positions, He must give me His grace, and in the most difficult, His grace is sufficient." – Hudson Taylor

1 Corinthians 15:10 "But by the remarkable grace of God I am what I am, and His grace toward me was not without effect. In fact, I worked harder than all of the apostles, though it was not I, but the grace of God, His unmerited favor and blessing which was with me."

This is a most impactful and powerful quote. Yet the problem is, do we believe it?

Since our birth, we have all had to understand, change, and develop. Well-being, contentment, and prolonged existence may be the payoffs for this. One fact is that from babyhood to adulthood, we evolve. We grow, and then we learn as we grow. But we still ponder our existence and why we are here.

So many of us have had some devastating experiences in life, and yet we are still pressing forward. We always say it is only by the grace of God that I am still here. This is one of the most factual statements anyone, believer or non-believer, can make. If not for the grace of our Lord, we would have perished.

Many years ago, I worked at a Lumber Company. One day, they were constructing a building while moving around the compound. I was walking alongside one of the Forman when a thick piece of metal fell from the structure's roof. We were not paying attention, although they yelled from above. I felt something hit the top of my head hard. In any other circumstances, I would have been killed. But because I was wearing a hard hat, the metal hit the hat and slid off to the right side of my shoulder. I was stunned for a couple of reasons. First, the metal's impact on my head made me dizzy. Second, I realized my life could have been over in that instance.

My first response should have been for me to say, "Thank You, Jesus!!!" But I didn't. We spent more time figuring out what went wrong than praising God for sparing my life. I thank God more now than I did then. I was spared.

A similar story happened to one of my friends in Texas. One morning, he went out jogging, and for the strangest of reasons, he entered a section where construction was going on, and a crane fell on him. He did not survive. Life is funny as we try to figure out how some things happen to one person, and they are spared life, yet when it happens to another, they are not. This is a segue to understanding God's grace and being thankful for it.

Let's go to the primary yet essential reason God extends His grace to us. God gave us grace so that we may provide it to others. We didn't deserve it, but God gave it to us anyway. Likewise, we are to extend grace to others, even if we do not think they deserve it. Jesus did not just die for us but also for all. He willingly went to the cross and failed to save us from our sins. He did it because He has genuine sacrificial love. It is known as the highest form of love because it's not artificial, made up, or unnatural. It is agape and is opened to, not closed off.

All of us experience God's grace daily, but few of us give Him thanks for it. If, for no other reason, we can think of to give God thanks for His grace, then let me give you one defined reason: It is through God's grace we are redeemed and freed from the grip of sin. This sin controlled us in this life. Through Christ's death, burial, and resurrection, we are saved. It is through his blood that forgiveness swallows our trespasses.

Because of whom He is, God gives completely, without restraint, and in abundance. He provides substantial grace because there can be no other way. Grace was given to us as a gift of love from God, not because we earned it, but because He has a good heart.

This is how we know, have, and understand grace: "God's life, power, and righteousness are given to us by unmerited favor." Through grace, God works to bring about an effective change in our hearts and lives. Grace gives us a life that God does not condemn.

Not just for Thanksgiving Day, be thankful, but be grateful every day for the grace of God. Because if we did not have

His grace, we would be destroyed.

Prayer: My Lord, we have so much to be grateful for. It is You who gave life to us. And we rejected You and Your ways. You still loved us enough that You did not give up on us. Thank You for this love that surpasses all understanding. It's because of Your great love we are eternal.

New Beginning, Same Result (Hopeful)

"God is so good to give us new days and New Years since He knows we need so many times to start over." – Lacey Sturm

2 Corinthians 7:1 says, "Since we have these promises, beloved, let us cleanse ourselves from every defilement of body and spirit, bringing holiness to completion in the fear of God."

A new year brings new beginnings, promises, resolutions, and expectations. We long to forget the past year and look forward to something fresh, original, and different. Too often, we forget to include God in our plans.

Without the newness of God in our lives and without thought, we embark on trying a new process to fix our problems. Yet, we still find ourselves stuck in the same place and getting the same results.

If we want a genuine change in our lives, we should give Jesus a chance to change it. The Bible tells us that if we are in Christ, if we are embedded in and joined to Him by our faith in Him, then we are already a new creature (2 Corinthians 5:17). The Holy Spirit regenerated and renewed us. What we once were or how we thought, be that morally and spiritually, have passed. Accepting Jesus as Lord and Savior will bring freshness and awaken our spirit with new life.

In addition, because of God's promises, we should allow changes that please God.

Start each new year as God has instructed us to. We should forget the former things and let go of contemplating the things of the past (Isaiah 43:18-20). If we are holding on to anything that is not good, we should consider letting it go, if we want a better life. Watch God do something new in our lives. If we are in God, we will see it come forth and be aware of it. Because He will build roads that we thought could never be built, and He will bring living water to our lives in dry and dead areas. New growth will prevail!

So, when each year ends, and before we make a promise that we will break or make a resolution that we will not keep, try putting our hope and trust in God. God, whose mercies are new every morning, is a keeper of promises. May everyone strive for a holy transformation, in Jesus, this New Year.

Prayer: Holy Father, as we have an opportunity to enter a New Year, please remind us to make You part of the promises and resolutions we will make to ourselves. Lord, You said that if we made a plan, you would design the path. So, please order our footsteps in Your Word, amen!

Why Isn't My Time for God Reciprocal? (Faithfulness)

"Time is free, but it's priceless. You can't own it, but you can use it. You can't keep it, but you can spend it. Once you've lost it, you can never get it back." – Harvey Mackay

2 Corinthians 8:5, 8, 24: "I say this not as a command, but to prove by the earnestness of others that your love also is genuine. So, give proof before the churches of your love and our boasting about you to these men. And this, not as we expected, but they gave themselves first to the Lord and then by the will of God to us."

Spending time with God can be a time to thank Him for the many blessings He has given us. We can grow closer to knowing who God is. We can develop a needed personal relationship with Him. Our interaction with Him will improve.

Why do we experience difficult moments when spending time with God? Is our flesh out maneuvering our Spirit? Do we feel that God listens to us? Do we question our Salvation? Simply put, do we know how to spend time with God?

We should try spending time with God, even when we are not in the mood. Don't just spend time with God; invest time with Him. If we want a fruitful walk with God, we must spend time with Him. Why is this still a struggle for many of us?

Some people believe God answers their prayers alone if they go to church. Some people think they have been redeemed from their sins because they know God and the Bible well.

One of the most common reasons we struggle to spend time with God is our fleshly pursuits (Romans 8:13). When we walk in the Spirit, we will have a relationship with God. Paul said if we live according to the flesh, then our minds are set on the things of the flesh. But if we live according to the Spirit, our minds are placed on the things of the Spirit. What are our minds set on? Are our views set on the things of this world? Or are our thoughts fixed on the things of God?

How strong is our desire to be with God? How are we viewing ourselves as responsible servants of God? What happens in our mind daily that keeps us from thinking about God? Whatever that may be, it may also be our struggle with desiring to be with Him. The apostle Paul put it in modest terms. He said some of us live according to the flesh because we set our minds on fleshly things. But those who live according to the Spirit have their minds set on the things of the Spirit (Ephesians 1:4).

God gives us all His love and time without ceasing. But we struggle with the reciprocation of that time. Since wanting to be near our Father is not our default, we fight our natural against our natural response to spend time with Him. Even when we have time, God, we don't choose that time to be with Him. It is truly up to us to set aside time for God. It is for our benefit.

My wife, Kim, is undoubtedly a "true" night owl. She does

her best work for God at 2 a.m. Yes, when I am cutting down a forest with my snoring, she is preparing a devotion, a speech, studying, or praying. I would walk in on her and find her head buried in the Bible. She often had a pen in hand and a pad nearby. But that is the time she has, and that is the time she gives back to God. Mark 1:35 tells us that Jesus rose early in the morning, left the house, and went to a special place to talk to God!

Many people fit this profile or get up early in the morning to read and study the Holy Bible, pray, and meditate. Others have set up a regiment that works for them. Whatever their sacrifice, they have chosen a time and set it aside for God. The time we respond to God happens because the Holy Spirit knows our schedule and the best time to get our attention. The people who have listened to the calling of the Holy Spirit made a bonified decision to give back some of the time God has given them! And they do it through prayer, praise, and serving.

With as much grace as our Heavenly Father extends to us daily, we should spend time with Him. We should invest time with our Lord. Suppose we struggle to give time back to God. In that case, we should begin praying that we make God the PRIORITY of our day and everything else secondary!

Prayer—Lord, Jesus, thank You for Your continuous forgiveness of our shortcomings, especially when it comes to You. You gave us Your all, and we have given only a little in return. Help us recognize You as first in our lives, and everything else will fall into place. It is in Your name we pray, amen!

A Unified Walk
(Faithfulness; Togetherness)

"The true self in unity with God always emanates from the interior of the heart." – Peter N. Borys

Ephesians 4:1-3 "I, therefore, a prisoner for the Lord, urge you to walk in a manner worthy of the calling to which you have been called, with all humility and gentleness, with patience, bearing with one another in love, eager to maintain the unity of the Spirit in the bond of peace."

Paul spoke to the Church of Corinth and warned the Church about being unequally yoked.

Being unequally yoked happens in more ways than just a relationship based on marriage. We may be unequally yoked due to our culture, the places we come from, the values we hold as true, and what we consider as norms.

As we enter into relationships, we will discover our many differences. We must evaluate the pros and cons of being in that relationship.

Of course, we could never overlook the fact that the "heart" knows what the heart wants, and we often pursue the desires of our heart.

Being unequally yoked can lead to a disproportionate relationship. We have a lot of people whose spiritual beliefs are so different that it creates many problems in their relationships. Those of us who follow Christ and find ourselves in a mismatched relationship are encouraged to remain in the relationship and walk in the way of Jesus to win the unbelieving individual over. Unless the two agree, they will not walk together.

Though we walk a separate path, having the love of God should help us walk together with those we disagree with. Consider the many friends we already have. Certainly, some of those friends have faiths different from ours, yet we have found a way to maintain the relationship (win them over).

So, how should those of us who have a calling in our lives walk? We should start every day with prayer. We should remember that we represent Christ in every way! We should meditate on God's Word as often as possible. We should establish spiritual boundaries so that we have lines drawn that we will never cross! And we should always remember what is essential and what is not.

We must understand that while walking in our calling, we serve the Lord, Jesus, and belong to Him. The method we use should complement our calling. On this graceful journey, our walk should be peaceful with perseverance, tenacity, and dedication, displaying love towards one another and a willingness to develop and keep the Spirit's harmony in a tranquil relationship.

Prayer: Heavenly Father, we seek You for strength. To walk with You is incredible, but the journey we take, at times, can be strenuous. So, we beg You to help us live and act in a way worthy of those chosen for such wonderful blessings as these. Help us be humble and gentle. Help us be patient, making room for each other's faults because of Your love. And help us follow the leading of the Holy Spirit. It's in Your name we pray, amen!

Even if I do not Ask, God Freely Gives (Generosity; Grace)

"Our confidence is not in what we have, but He who freely gave us what we have. If God's will is in your little stones, they will surely bring down giant Goliaths... but you have to make the throw!" – Israelmore Ayivor

John 1:16 "And from his fullness we have all received, grace upon grace."

We understand that grace is an unanticipated gift from our Lord to us. It is how our God expresses His kindness. It cost us nothing. Capricious and unmerited. We often say we received favor from God when these instances occur. One of God's characteristics is demonstrated in the redemption of all sinners because even the non-believer receives grace from God.

Why didn't God just set His grace aside for those who believe in Him? Well, that would mean none of us would be alive. We are not born into believing in the existence of God. We come to believe in Him in many ways, and we are saved through the blood of Jesus Christ if we accept Him as our Lord and Savior.

So, grace is necessary for all our survival here on Earth, lest many perish without ever having an opportunity to receive salvation.

God's grace to us differs from the grace we extend to others. We go wrong by setting restrictions or may even have an ulterior motive for extending grace. We are broken, lost, and sinful, so our dignity cannot compare to God's grace.

God has displayed His grace by saving us because we cannot save ourselves. We will not have to face agony and suffering in Hell. Jesus took the painful death, so we don't have to. And because of His actions, we have been reconciled unto God, and we will go to Heaven.

But what about the more straightforward ways God has extended grace to us? He gave us our spouses and children. God did not give up on us, even when we "snubbed" Him time after time. He either spared us or saved us from abuse. God gave us a vehicle to help us go to many places we need to travel to. He gave us a home that supplied a roof over our heads. God gave us a nice warm bed to sleep in and clothes to wear. He provided us with jobs to help us take care of our families. He even helped some of us overcome some tough medical challenges. Do I need to say more?

So why does God continuously give us grace upon grace? John 1:16 tells us that Jesus is full of grace, and we constantly receive more grace. Christ is full of grace, and those who believe in Him get showered with grace. We received spiritual blessing upon spiritual blessings. We receive favor upon favor. And we receive gifts upon gifts. What is undoubtedly clear is that when we come to Jesus, He dishes out grace in tremendous ways.

If we have friends, we want to share what we know about God's grace with them. If our friends do not know Jesus as their personal Lord and Savior, do not create ways to push them away from the hope everyone should have in Christ for salvation. Before Jesus found and saved us, we did not consider anything about our eternity. But God extended His grace to us. Therefore, we should extend that same grace to our friends.

Prayer: Heavenly Father, we come before You with a heart of gratefulness. Thank You for sharing Your grace that keeps us filled with Your Spirit! We will never forget the blessing You pour into our lives daily! And please help us do the same towards the people we meet daily. Amen!

Easter, The Reason We Celebrate (Sacrifice-Season)

"We aren't called to shine our own light; we are called to reflect His."

Philippians 3:10: "I want to know Christ—yes, to know the power of his resurrection and participation in his sufferings, becoming like him in his death."

Happy Easter, everyone. I pray that you find even more reason to celebrate our risen savior, Jesus Christ, on this day.

I want to share a scripture and a small message about Easter.

1 Peter 1:3 Blessed be the God and Father of our Lord Jesus Christ! According to his great mercy, he has caused us to be born again to a living hope through the resurrection of Jesus Christ from the dead.

Easter is another holiday observed by Christians and others worldwide, yet it is controversial. However, we will not focus on the controversies. Instead, let us take a moment to see how some other cultures celebrate this wonderful and magnificent day.

In Spain, people observe Easter for an entire week on their peninsula. Festivities commence throughout the last week of Lent, and observations are made by recognizing enormous and sophisticated religious parades in nearly every part of the country.

In France, Easter customs stem from Catholic customs and are usually a more sacred affair than in the UK. One practice is to stop ringing church bells around Easter out of respect for Jesus's death.

In Germany, Good Friday and Easter are considered public holidays. On Holy Saturday, people rejoice by lighting bonfires around sunset. Other practices include beautifying an "Easter tree" with hand-painted eggs. Usually, families drape the adornments from a small household tree.

In Italy, the Pope leads the Easter celebrations. On Good Friday, a gigantic mass is held at St. Peter's. During the mass, a vast crucifix is raised, lighting up the night sky.

And there is Bermuda. Here, Easter is more easygoing. Bermudians of all ages celebrate Good Friday on the beach, flying both unique homemade and store-bought kites, which supposedly represent Christ's resurrection.

Let us take a mini-detail look at what occurs in America: Many Americans attend church. Most offer special programming for this service. Some even organize a special brunch for the congregation and guests. After providing their praises to God and fellowshipping with their friends and neighbors, they continue festivities by having an Easter egg hunt for the children. Most of all, we eat a lot.

I am so happy to see many cultures celebrate Easter in different ways. It is great to see when people come together for a great reason. I am sure it puts a big smile on God's face when His children gather in His name and the name of His Son.

But let us ensure we send the correct message to everyone celebrating Easter. When we think about Easter, the things we have fun doing are by-products of why we do it.

So, when it comes to Easter, we love to think about baskets filled with candy, elegant hats, our imaginative Easter bunny, and eggs of different sorts. These things bring temporary happiness to a temporary moment in our lives, and we are grateful to God for it.

We also make sure to celebrate Easter in this season because of Jesus, who died and rose from the dead.

We commemorate this special day to revere our infinitely perfect God, who removed Himself from all divinity by deciding to give up His rights and life to reestablish and save our lives.

God did not wish to punish us, and we did not get what we deserved. Instead, He showed us His love in a wonderful way. He sent Jesus to us to give us a second chance.

Jesus took on the gloomiest evils of this world and experienced the worst death for all of us. He is why we celebrate Easter.

So please enjoy this day and celebrate it. For all that it brings to us, remember the reason we have for the celebration.

Prayer: Lord Jesus, thank You for making the ultimate sacrifice for all of us and forgiving those who didn't even realize it. It's only because of You that we even have life. It is in Your name we pray, amen!

Putting The Rudder Back On Your Ship (Faith)

"A man without a purpose is like a ship without a rudder." – Thomas Carlyle

Psalm 107:29 "He made the storm be still, and the waves of the sea were hushed."

How did we traverse our way through the COVID-19 period? That is a funny question because some of us did not navigate at all. Some of us did not move before COVID-19 invaded our land; and even in a post-COVID era, we still have not moved. We have let our rudder separate from our ship. Our ship is our purpose in life. Since then, we have been floating in the water without any direction, as if the wind had left our sail.

When COVID-19 struck the United States, it was so devastating to our country because we acted as if we had never faced an epidemic before. But as a reminder, we have always had pandemics/epidemics throughout the centuries: Smallpox in the 1600s, Yellow Fever in the 1700s, Cholera and Scarlet Fever in the 1800s, Bird Flu, Typhoid Mary, Measles, Spanish Flu, Swine Flu, Polio, Aids/HIV, and Diphtheria in the 1900s, and Whooping Cough, and COVID-19 in the 2000s, and we are still early in this century. Look at what we have been through as a country and overcome. We responded, then, like we did with COVID.

At what point did we allow our rudder to separate from our ship? Was it the information reported by the news, broadcast by the radio, or written in the newspaper? Was it our neighbor, who consistently talked about the effects of the virus, who convinced us to start living like a recluse (Genesis 2:18)? What were the defining words we heard that persuaded us to say, "I am just going to stop living?"

We forgot that we are the ships of God and that He is the rudder. No matter the type of storm, God knows how to steer us through it. When we take control of the helm of our ship, we separate ourselves from God. This separation causes us to have doubts and weakens our faith. We no longer depend on Him but only on ourselves.

Suppose we recognize that we have lost our rudder during this pandemic. In that case, we need to find it and reconnect with it so our ship can begin sailing in the direction God wants it to go. Essentially, we must return to God and do the work He has called perform to do. We need to let our sails, which are the winds of God, take us where He is leading. We must not act like the disciples when Jesus slept, giving away to anxiety and fear, but we must remain calm during the storm. Was it, not He who caused it, and it is also He who will return it to a peaceful state (Isaiah 45:7)!

Prayer: Gracious Father, forgive us when we decide to separate from You. Point us back to You so that our lives will have purpose and we will see clear direction from You. It is in Your name I pray, amen!

Why We Don't Rest During the Storm (Faith)

"Serenity isn't the peace away from the storm; it's the peace at the eye of the storm." – Ed Martin

Psalm 57:1 "Be merciful to me, O God, be merciful to me, for in you my soul takes refuge; in the shadow of your wings, I will take refuge till the storms of destruction pass by."

We always head for shelter when we see a storm approaching. No one wants to face the fury of a hurricane.

Hurricanes are the most powerful storm known to people. It is through hurricanes that strong wind form. Floods surge. Rain falls brutally. Deadly tornadoes can grow. Fast-moving water overcomes the coast. These are just a few things that come with a devastating storm! No wonder we head for cover! Very few people can survive the fury of a storm unless they take up safety in a shelter!

Jesus was sleeping through a storm below deck when the apostles rushed to wake Him. A great storm was upon them, yet Jesus was sleeping through it. That concerned the disciples, who saw it as Jesus not caring. Well, Jesus, in all His glory, woke and commanded the storm to be still. What we learned is that the winds stopped instantly. The apostles recognized that even the waters and the winds obeyed Jesus' command. Yet they still lacked faith!

Some of our lives are in a wreck because we have faced many storms, yet we have not run for cover. Some of us pray to God to cease the storms, yet we consistently try to shield ourselves from them by human means. We verbally pray to God, yet in our hearts, some of us believe God does nothing. We take full responsibility because the problems are in front of us, and we hastily turn within ourselves to resolve the issues.

Day by day, difficulties seem to "pound" us relentlessly from every angle. Yet, we refuse to hand the problems entirely over to God. We must keep a handle on the situation because we still want to be in control.

The storms of our lives come in the form of tribulations, and Jesus is our shelter. If Jesus can calm the storms of winds and waters, then He can calm the storms of our lives. Jesus is the completion of all God promises. He is our rock and our stronghold. Jesus is our shelter, and the Lord is a place we can dwell during times of hardship. He is our cry for rescue and relief. If He had the power to rescue us from sin and death, then surely, He can rescue us from life's problems.

Depending on the situation, it is hard for me to remain still. But God commands all of us to be still and know He is God! If we do this, we can rest peacefully and let the storm pass over us.

Prayer: Lord Jesus, we are thankful that we have You to call upon us during the stormy seasons of our lives. Please remain merciful and keep us at peace during our challenging times. Amen.

My Life Has Been Shaped by My Thoughts
(Trust; Faith; Belief)

"We are what our thoughts have made us, so take care of what you think. Words are secondary. Thoughts live; they travel far." – Swami Vivekananda

Psalm 139:23-24 "Search me, O God, and know my heart! Try me and know my thoughts! And see if there be any grievous way in me, and lead me in the way everlasting!"

Like many others, I was not always proud of how I conducted myself growing up. In most cases, I would respond to things out of anger. I did not love being angry about things, but it became a place of comfort for me as I trusted my angry ways more than anything else. Yet, at the same time, I did not want to be in that place.

After many unfortunate incidents and situations, I looked at myself. I told myself that I could have handled it better. But when these opportunities presented themselves, I still did not humble myself. And I could not figure out why. This way of living went on for many years, as I would confront people about things they often were right about. But because it differed from my thought, I felt it was wrong.

I know I am not the only one who goes through this emotion, but I am alone when dealing with this internal issue. I struggled with the need to always be right. I hated losing arguments and refused to admit defeat. I needed to have the last word, and when I didn't, I became angrier.

It was very apparent that I needed a changed heart. What I didn't realize was it was going to be one of those long-life lessons. Over time, God placed me in many situations where I opposed others when they spoke. Being in opposition is not a bad thing. It is more important how we handle conflict.

During this same period, I learned that I could not be all God wanted me to be until I learned how to have better relationships with others. I know how I felt was influenced by what I had gone through. And, often, these were things I had no control over. My feelings and my thoughts were always conflicting. My feelings in my heart were one way, but my thoughts caused me to go in a different direction. The thoughts in my head had more impact than the feelings I felt in my heart.

But God pointed out to me in Proverbs 4:23 to be careful how I thought because my thoughts shaped my life. Even if those thoughts weren't true, I still believed them, and it affected my thinking and impacted my life. I needed to work on controlling the many circumstances I found myself in If I was going to get my life going in a positive direction.

So, I decided to hand my life to God so He could help me with my thinking. Romans 12:2 told me to let God transform me into a new person by changing my thoughts. Not only did I need a new life, but I desperately wanted one.

It is worse to run away from an opposing view, so we must stand when called to. In facing opposition, I had to find a better way to convey what I felt and why I felt the way I did it. The Bible tells us to disagree in love. It's okay to disagree, but how we handle it is essential. I didn't want my life filled with angry thoughts about good people, so this change had to occur. Again, during this period, it became more critical for me to be heard than for me to be right!

Prayer: Father, thank You so much for Your patience with us. We know that we can be challenging at times. Still, please continue to work on our thoughts to match the feelings in my heart, and we can be a better person to Your people and a better servant for You. Amen.

God Is My Shepherd, Yet I Still Want (Needs; Generosity)

"Everyone has some darkness inside. It's like a hungry creature. It wants and wants and wants with a terrible power." – Jeanne DuPrau

Genesis 9:3 "Every moving thing that lives shall be food for you. And as I gave you the green plants, I give you everything."

Some people are content with life and do not desire more than they already have. Others, regardless of what they have, still want more. Those who are fortunate do not know how blessed they are until someone less fortunate comes alone. And those who are unfortunate will not recognize it until someone who has more comes alone.

I can testify to that as a kid because I did not realize my family's shortcomings until I started attending school. In most cases, other children's clothes and shoes were better than mine.

I have appreciated God's sprinkling of blessings in my life. I never get too much at once, but it is just enough to be thankful for. These became great expressions of God's grace and love. It has placed me in a state of not wanting more but having a heart of acceptance of the things that He gives me. In other words, I lack for nothing. It is a great place to be when we realize God provides for all our needs (James 1:4).

So, why do we still want if all our needs are covered? Can it possibly be that we are overlooking God's provision because of our personal desires? Could it be that God may give in a different way than we hope for? Did it mean we could do whatever we wanted when God set us free? Not! We can live by the rules of sin, or we can live by God's rules; there are no others. So many times, when God does something great for us, we still find a reason to complain.

We often ask God to give us more of Him. It is in our words, in our prayers, and in the songs that we sing. But wanting more of God means having less of ourselves. We would have to give up more of who we are to have more of who God is. You remember the saying, "May I be decreased, Lord, so that you may be increased?" Did we mean it, or is it just for show? Seeking God's kingdom first is our primary function. We should seek Him before we seek other things. But we often seek out different things and then ask God to give those things to us.

God provides for us in ways we do not understand. He does this because He cares for us. Think about this: If we care for our children and do everything possible to provide for them, don't we believe God will do the same thing and more for us?

We question God about many things because when He does things, it just does not look right in our own eyes. God does things so that He can be seen, not just in our eyes but also in the eyes of others.

When we give our children gifts, sometimes they do not understand why we gave them a gift they needed instead of a gift they wanted. Case in point: One Christmas, I bought all three of our daughters a safety kit for their vehicles. They all chuckled at the kit at first. But they all had to use their kits, especially during the wintertime, whether it was to help others or to help themselves. So, what is the lesson here? We can trust God's provision, even when it looks awkward in our eyes.

Prayer: Lord, please help us be more appreciative of what You give us! Help us understand that the things You provide us are more beneficial than what we want. It is in Your name we pray, amen!

Striking the Rock in Anger (Self Control)

"For every minute you remain angry, you give up sixty seconds of peace of mind."
– Ralph Waldo Emerson

Psalm 37:8 "Refrain from anger, and forsake wrath! Fret not yourself; it tends only to evil."

How many times have we missed the opportunity to let God's glory be revealed because of our selfish acts? As we travel in this life's journey, God gives us many opportunities to show Him to others. Yet, we consistently fall short of the revelation of God's glory because of our thinking and our feelings. When the pressures of life become overwhelming, it could be hard for us to follow God's command. These pressures often cause us to fail to do what God has called us to and how he wants us to do it (1 John 5:3). In addition, God's commandments are indeed able for us to manage.

1 John 5:30 makes me think of Moses. Even great servants of God often fell short of God's commands. In Numbers 20:8, God gave Moses and Aaron a simple command - "Take the rod, and you and your brother Aaron assemble the congregation and speak to the rock before their eyes, that it may yield its water. You shall thus bring forth water for them out of

the rock and let the congregation and their beasts drink." However, because of Moses' frustrations with the people, he took matters into his own hands. Numbers 20:10-11 reveal that Moses and Aaron gathered the assembly before the rock. And he said to them, "Listen now, you rebels; shall we bring forth water for you out of this rock?" Then Moses lifted his hand and struck the rock twice with his rod, and water came forth abundantly, and the congregation and their beasts drank. Because of his feelings and actions, Moses received the credit instead of God receiving it. At this point, Moses becomes fed up with the people.

Although earlier, God did instruct Moses to strike the rock. Nevertheless, God gave Moses a new set of instructions, and Moses disobeyed God's command. Moses paid a heavy price for his disobedience. God did not permit Moses to cross over into the promised land.

How many of us are missing the opportunities to enter the many blessings of God because we fail to follow the instructions He gives to us? We love others seeing and hearing us, and we love that we are the center of attraction. But in doing so, we may block the revelation of God's glory and receive the credit for ourselves.

I wish I could say that I have always followed God's instructions with a loving heart in obeying God, but I have not. Sometimes, I did things angrily because it was what He willed, but not what I wanted. I had found it very difficult to show love towards others who were not loving towards me. However, in moments like these, God wants to shine the brightest through us. We learn this in James 1:20-For man's anger does not produce the righteousness of God.

God encourages us to praise one another, but God should always be at the center of our lives in everything we do. Let us pray that we yield to the will of God and obey His command by following and executing those commands in the way He wants us to display them.

Following God's obedience comes the promises of God if we do not strike the rock but speak to it. 2 Peter 1:4 says, "And because of his glory and excellence, has given great and precious promises. These promises enable you to share God's divine nature and escape the world's corruption caused by human desires.

Prayer: Jesus, when You came, You became an example for all of us. We know sometimes our anger is justified, but You have asked us not to sleep with anger in our hearts. Please help us to resolve our anger so that we can have a peaceful rest. Amen!

Reaching Out in Love During Difficult Times (Suffering; Hardship)

"On the other side of a storm is the strength that comes from having navigated through it. Raise your sail and begin." — Gregory S. Williams

Romans 8:18 "For I consider that the sufferings of this present time are not worth comparing with the glory to be revealed to us."

Sometimes, we can be dismayed when we look at disappointing things. But in honoring the Great Commission, Jesus gave us a task, which is what we must keep at hand. The Lord commissioned believers to go out and share about Him. However, we needed to understand the difficulty that we would experience in doing so. Remember the many followers of Christ who had callous times serving. Like the disciples, we can take many roads in our travels and speak to many people about what we were taught.

Life does not stop simply because we are serving God. In some aspects, it becomes harder. Following Jesus' command and serving God can be very demanding and draining. As we honor Jesus, we must remember that it's not about the number of people we encounter; it's about the number that accepts Him. All the Angels of heaven will rejoice if one person accepts Jesus as Lord (Luke 15:10)!

What we learn about God is that we will have pain and suffering. God did not spare His servants or Jesus. Through their suffering, we see God's power and true love!

The Book of Joel describes the pain we experience, which can feel like God's fierce anger. But this pain serves to reveal God's warm compassion toward us. Joel tells us that, through our pain, God still has gracious, merciful, abounding, and steadfast love for us. He relents over our pain, agony, and suffering. He gives in to us when we are in torment, torture, and facing many tribulations. God still reaches out to us and extends His love. And He expects us to do the same.

Remember Jesus suffering on the cross. He never lashed out in anger in all His agony and pain. Instead, Jesus continued to reach out in love. He even asked God to forgive those torturing Him because they did not understand what they were doing (Luke 23:34). What an incredible display of love.

Sometimes, our pain can prevent us from extending love to others. We must learn to embrace the pain we have yet to show the love of God to all who need it. When people see this display, they will begin to understand. We may be on the short end of receiving love from others, but let us not be short of giving it.

Prayer: Father, sometimes we hurt so badly that we do not want to love others. In those times, we need You to help us overcome our pain so that others will understand the true nature of agape love. It is in Your mighty name we pray, amen!!!

This Duty is Beneath Me
(Kindness, Love)

"Do not keep away from the measure which has no limit, or from the task which has no end." — Rabbi Tarphon

John 13:14-17 "So, if I, the Lord, and the Teacher, washed your feet, you should also wash one another's feet. I gave you this as an example, so you should do in turn as I did to you. I assure you and most solemnly say that a slave is not greater than his master, nor is sent more significant than the one who sent him. If you know these things, you are blessed, happy, and favored by God if you put them into practice and faithfully do them."

When my family and I arrived in Bemidji, one of our favorite stores was Dollar Tree. It was our beloved store the first year as we tried to get settled in and become accustomed to the culture and the weather.

After a year, when the girls attained more secure jobs, their taste in where they shopped changed. No one changed more than Paige, our oldest. Kim and I still frequent Dollar Tree. Our two younger daughters made some visits but have yet to cut them off completely. But Paige does not go near the Dollar Tree at all now. We always joke with Paige about her becoming snobbish and seeing Dollar Tree as a store beneath her.

As we joke with Paige about this situation, this is true for many people. Some of us feel what God asked us to do is beneath us.

Having too much wealth is a foundational reason for some people becoming snobs. They brag about themselves and their successes while looking down on others. They make it a point to avoid certain people. They want people to believe they are more appealing and ambitious than anyone else.

Snooty people have some very annoying traits that are easy to identify. They criticize the choices you make in life. They ensure people know about them by broadcasting their day-to-day lives on social media. They are very obsessed with labels and talk about money a lot. They believe they are the most essential and are often not very friendly. They are very selfish and try to enforce their point of view upon others. They love putting others down. They consider others beneath them if they do not have as much as they have! And one other thing, they will not labor with their own hands. They will pay others to do it. In other words, they do not want to get dirty or deal with anything they consider filthy.

Before life changed, I remember not having money, wearing the same clothes for two or three days, and driving a car with a big hole in the floor. If you sat in the back of the vehicle, you would see the road as I drove my car.

How do we manage to do jobs God called us to perform, but in our hearts and minds, we tell ourselves, this is beneath me, or I did not sign up for this! Sometimes, we may have to talk to people with open sores or who smell unbelievably bad. The places we travel may not be clean. People may only have an unappealing fragrance. We may be called to go to some of these places as someone who serves God. We must go because these places are where some of the people we must talk to lives.

Now, let us reflect on Jesus, performing the common task of washing the dirty and stinky feet of His disciples. Peter tried to stop Jesus from washing his feet because Peter felt this action was beneath our Lord. Washing the disciples' feet did not contradict Christ as Master. It drew a hard line challenging our ordinary sense of what leadership truly means. It established the shared love and support Jesus displayed as fundamental to living out the Christian faith.

Jesus explained that when the master performs a task, servants do not get to dismiss that same action as "beneath them." He crushes the standard of "that's beneath me." Jesus Christ worked in humility and service to others. Regardless of our positions in life, we have no right to turn up our noses to serve others. To do so suggests we are "too good" to do for others what Christ did for us.

Prayer: Lord, Jesus, in our desire to be more like You, please help us by giving us more understanding. Too often, we want You to do things that would satisfy us but not bring You glory! We need to remember. You walked miles and slept in the dirt on Your many journeys. But help us not forget that You, God, knelt to wash other men's feet. Teach us that kind of humbleness so that we can avoid unnecessary resentment and having a sense of entitlement. Amen!

When God Derails Our Plan
(Faith; Patience; Trust)

"What we plan for ourselves isn't always what life has planned for us."

Malachi 3:6: "For I the Lord do not change; therefore you, O children of Jacob, are not consumed."

For many years, my wife and I took vacation trips in August. Every time we got ready to return home, we both complained about how much we hated traveling through Atlanta, Georgia. It was such a stressful time. We needed to get used to how fast people drove and how their thought process differed than ours, as it related to driving.

One year, while traveling, God heard our hearts and our prayers. When we were getting ready to return home from Florida, the GPS immediately directed us to take another route. It was very, very odd. We had traveled the same path for many years and had planned to return the same way. We started traveling west on Highway 27 and connected with Highway 84, which took us right into Alabama. I looked at my wife and said, "Boo, there is something wrong with your GPS; we just entered Alabama."

She rechecked the route and said, "No, it shows us heading

in the right direction." I responded, "Okay, we will continue to follow, but I guess at some point, we'll get pulled back east to go through Atlanta."

So, after many hours of driving and still not feeling comfortable on this current route, I asked my wife to recheck the GPS because we had just passed the ramp to Atlanta. My wife, getting a little irritated now, responded, "Don't you think the GPS knows where it is taking us?" I took that as she wanted me to keep driving.

When leaving Tallahassee, Florida, and traveling to Nashville, Tennessee, we always took the same route. It was what we knew and what we were familiar with. But we complained about being on that route all the time. If only we could get around Atlanta, we would take it. Our few stops took us about nine hours to arrive in Nashville. I looked back at our trip and asked, "How did that happen?"

When God begins changing the course in our life, we do as much as we can to hold off that change because it is a change we are not familiar with, we are not comfortable with it, and we cannot see how we are going to arrive to where we are trying to go.

No matter how much we complain, we do not want to change. Sometimes, He just wants to snap us out of that state of complacency of comfort we all live in. When God makes a change, it is for our benefit and His glory.

Even though God changes things in our lives, His Word does not change. But God does change His mind. He did it many times in the Bible, from changing the route the Israelites were traveling during the exodus to no longer accepting the sacrifice of burnt offerings to adding 15 years to King Hezekiah's life. God can and will change His mind about many things without changing anything about His Word.

Aren't we glad that God does change His mind about certain things? How many of us would still be around if He did not?

God changed His mind about destroying the world. How do we know this? He sent His only Son to save us, and we are the reason He spared us.

So, when our plan starts going in a direction we did not plan, we should thank God in advance because He knows much more about where He wants to take us than we do.

Prayer: Father of all the heavens, what a privilege it is for us to be in Your presence. Lord, Your Word tells us to prepare, but You would be the one who orders our footsteps. No matter how we plan, help us always follow the path You have designed for us each day. It's in Your name we pray, amen!

LIVING WITHIN GOD'S GRACE!

There are two gifts God has given to everyone without any requirements from us. It is "Grace" and "Mercy!" Since they are something that we don't have to work for, we give very little thought to either of them.

God's mercy and His grace exist all around us, every day!

He has given us His mercy because He has chosen not to punish us, but to allow us an opportunity to repent of our disobedience towards Him. He did this on the greatest scale of love people have ever known, through the sacrifice of His own son's life. It was a heavy price to pay, but Jesus carried that cost to the cross.

And there is God's grace. God's grace is defined as undeserved favor. For us, it means it cannot be earned. God gives it to us freely. Having God's grace allows us the chance to build a spiritual and personal relationship with Him.

Each day, God extends grace to us. Jesus lived and practiced grace when He walked among us. It is incumbent upon us to reciprocate this same grace by forgiving others who have done wrong to us.

During the past few years, I have learned much about the importance of grace. This journey has taught me much. I see what grace has done for me, and I observe what grace does for others when I extend it. Not only has it brought a change in my heart, but a change in my life. God has shown me why grace is important to Him. And now, it is just as important to me!!!